SAYING I DO

TO A
SUCCESSFUL
MARRIAGE

300+ QUESTIONS TO BUILD
A REWARDING, HAPPY, AND
INTIMATE RELATIONSHIP

CIDER MILL
PRESS

BOOK
PUBLISHERS
KENNEBUNKPORT, MAINE

Alexandra Carley & Shane Carley

Say "I Do" To A Successful Marriage

13-Digit ISBN: 978-1-64643-001-7
10-Digit ISBN: 1-64643-001-8

This book may be ordered by mail from the publisher. Please include $5.99
for postage and handling. Please support your local bookseller first!
Books published by Cider Mill Press Book Publishers are available at special discounts
for bulk purchases in the United States by corporations, institutions, and other
organizations. For more information, please contact the publisher.

Cider Mill Press Book Publishers
"Where good books are ready for press"
PO Box 454
12 Spring Street
Kennebunkport, Maine 04046
Visit us online
cidermillpress.com

Typography: Brandon Grotesque, Thistails

Printed in Singapore
1 2 3 4 5 6 7 8 9 0
First Edition

Table of Contents

INTRO-DUCTION

Before deciding to walk down the aisle, you and your significant other likely covered the biggies: Do you want kids? Do we share the same core values? But what about the questions that impact your day-to-day lives together on a smaller scale, like your ideal morning routine, your preferred amount of alone time, or what makes you feel most appreciated? How about a new skill you'd like to master together as a couple? We've curated a year's worth of conversation starters like these for couples at the beginning of their marriage.

"THE MEETING OF TWO PERSONALITIES IS LIKE THE CONTACT OF TWO CHEMICAL SUBSTANCES: **IF THERE IS ANY REACTION, BOTH ARE TRANSFORMED.**"

~Carl Jung

SOME OF THE QUESTIONS ARE STRAIGHTFORWARD—
questions about personel preferences, childhood, and aspirations.
Others are more thought-provoking, intended to make you both sit
back and consider something on a deeper level. For the questions that
sit somewhere in between, we decided to offer a brief annotation,
elaborating on our intention behind the conversation starter at hand.
For instance, "How much fulfillment do you need from your job?" may
seem uncomplicated—perhaps your sense of purpose at work is of vital
importance, or maybe you just need a paycheck to fund the after-work
hobbies that gratify you. Whatever the response, understanding where
your partner lands on this seemingly small detail can be essential as you
navigate how best to support them through work-related milestones
or transitions, or even how to avoid imposing your own career-related
expectations on your spouse. We hope the annotations that we've
woven throughout make for more meaningful conversations, or at least
give you a different path to a topic that you've perhaps already
explored together.

The questions fall into five different categories, each designed to
make you think about a different aspect of your relationship and your
lives together.

HABITS AND HOBBIES: What do you like to do together? Perhaps more importantly, what does your partner like to do on their own? Answering such questions will help you do a better job of spending time together, and apart, in a way you both enjoy.

SEX AND INTIMACY: Sex is an important part of any marriage, but being intimate and vulnerable with your partner can come in many different forms. Learning more about your partner's preferences when it comes to intimacy is important.

FAMILY AND FRIENDS: Some people have a great relationship with their partner's family and friends, while others struggle with those connections. Understanding how your partner interacts with the people who are most important to you—and why—can help you understand who they are as a person.

GOALS AND ASPIRATIONS: Hopefully you've already discussed the broad strokes of your life goals by the time you're getting married, but there are always smaller goals to be identified. You never know, you and your partner might discover you've both secretly always wanted goats and chickens!

QUIRKS AND SCRUPLES: Do you whistle while you work? Does your partner pace the house while they brush their teeth? It's nice to have an excuse to bring up minor annoyances—or even to tell your spouse how cute it is when they hum while washing dishes.

THE HEAVY STUFF: You're just setting out on what hopefully is a long and happy marriage. But the unexpected is inevitable. These questions broach topics that aren't fun to think about, although they are important.

The process of getting to know your partner doesn't stop the day you say "I do," and nor should it. We're constantly evolving, in big and small ways. Our priorities shift, we embrace new interests, confront unexpected challenges, take on new responsibilities at work or change careers altogether. A knee-jerk "How was your day?" may keep you up to date with your partner's most immediate, front-of-mind pre-occupations, but it doesn't necessarily open the door to the deeper conversations that keep you connected in a more meaningful way. Those deep-dive questions don't always spring forth naturally, so we've curated a balance of thought-provoking questions that ask you and your partner to turn inward, as well as lighter conversation-starters and "would you rather" scenarios that simply serve as a fun way to discover something new about what makes your partner tick.

When people ask us what the key to our relationship is, we always give the same answer: communication. This isn't a secret, nor is it any great revelation that communication is important to a relationship, but communication means more than just talking to one another. It means having the confidence to tackle subjects that aren't necessarily fun, topics that you know might lead to a difficult or intense conversation. It also means making your partner feel comfortable having those conversations with you, knowing that they won't be judged for their answers. Keeping those lines of communication open is a good thing in its own right, but it also helps set an open and positive tone for your interactions—and your relationship—as a whole.

One of the joys of marriage is that no matter how long you've been together, there is always something new to learn about your partner.

So flip to any page and dive in!

"SHARED JOY IS
A DOUBLE JOY;
SHARED SORROW IS
HALF A SORROW."

~Swedish Proverb

HABITS AND HOBBIES

Launching a new phase in your partnership can be a
great opportunity to check in on the quotidian habits
that you take for granted, or even commit to new
routines together. Being thoughtful about how your
interests and natural rhythms align with those of
your spouse can help you discover new ways to spend
quality time with each other, or even just approach
your daily life together with more intention.

Describe your perfect relaxing weekend.

How much alone time do you need in a given day, and when do you need it most?

What is your ideal morning routine?

What's your ideal bedtime?

How much sleep do you need to feel rested?

This may not feel like the most personal question, but the amount of sleep people need can vary greatly. Some people can stay up until 1 a.m. and wake up for work at 6 a.m. feeling perfectly rested. Others might go to bed at 9 p.m. and still struggle to rouse themselves when the alarm goes off at 7 a.m. There's no guarantee that you and your partner will have perfectly compatible sleep schedules. Understanding the other's needs can help you give them a little more consideration. Maybe that means letting them sleep in a little later on weekends, or asking them to walk the dog while you catch a few extra Z's. It's an opportunity to be just a little more mindful of your partner's needs.

How do you prefer to unwind after work?

Are there any chores you just hate to do, or those you really don't mind at all?

What activities do we tend to engage in separately, that you wish we did together?

What's your favorite part of a typical weekday in our lives (even if it's something mundane)?

It's fun to consider things you don't often have a reason to think about. Maybe your partner brushes their teeth while you shower, and you enjoy those few minutes of intimacy and conversation that you wouldn't otherwise get. Or maybe your partner always kisses you goodbye before leaving for work, or kisses you goodnight before bed. Maybe it's as simple as the fact that they always do the dishes because they know you hate that particular chore. It's always nice to let your partner know that they are appreciated, even if it's for little things that you might not think about very often.

How often should we have
wine or beer with dinner?

Do you like staying up
and sleeping in later than
usual on the weekends, or
would you rather maintain
our weekday rhythms?

If we joined
a club or
organization in
our community
together, what
would it be?

Is there a podcast that you listen to or a show that you watch solo that you wish we engaged in together?

Are there certain times that are sacred to you, like your morning routine, Saturday brunch, or Sunday football?

Is it important to you that we eat meals together?

For some families, meals represent important quality time when everyone gathers together. For other families, meals just happen to be when we eat, and might be spent in front of the television or even entirely separate. How you prefer to spend mealtimes isn't something you would necessarily think to ask a partner, but you might be surprised by how much having a partner who doesn't share your point of view can affect your happiness. Taking the time to discuss these seemingly small preferences can go a long way toward ensuring that you are both on the same page for these daily rituals.

Do you enjoy cooking? If so, what is your favorite meal to prepare?

How often should we change the sheets?

Is there anything you enjoy that you're just a little bit embarrassed about?

When you want to treat yourself to something decadent, what's your go-to?

Everyone has a guilty pleasure, and although a lot of people will answer "chocolate," "wine," or something similar, it doesn't have to be limited to food. Maybe you treat yourself to some nice new clothes or buy a video game you've been wanting to play. Finding out what your partner reaches for when they feel like treating themselves provides ample gift ideas. If you know your partner loves tiramisu, you might celebrate a big work accomplishment by getting them some, or better yet, making it yourself!

Are there any tasks or chores that you handle regularly that you wish I stepped in and helped with?

What is your favorite restaurant experience that we've had together?

What do you do when
you can't sleep?

What is your favorite day
of the week, and why?

Do you consider yourself a planner or do you prefer to be more spontaneous?

Do you make "to-do" lists for yourself?

Are there any spiritual or religious activities that are important to you?

What aspects of our marriage do you feel you should be able to take for granted?

We've all had different relationship dynamics modeled for us by our parents, our friends, our siblings, previous relationships, and even the media we consume. Everyone's lived experience is different, and what may seem like a given to one person could be perceived as "above and beyond" to another. Discussing the parts of your daily routines that may seem too small to mention can actually shed light on the things that are most important to you in your married life.

Name a behavior or habit that you've grown out of and are happy to have left behind.

Is there a task that you always prefer to do yourself?

Is it important to you that we go to bed at the same time?

Do you think we divide and conquer household chores equitably?

Do you have any bad habits that you are actively trying to break?

Are there any healthy habits you would like to try to cultivate?

"I want to be healthier" is a goal that a lot of people share, from eating better, fostering a more positive mindset, hitting the gym more often, or numerous other interpretations. But it's hard to develop a new habit on your own. Having a partner to help keep you accountable or even tackle the problem with you can make the difference between starting a healthy new habit and letting it fall by the wayside. Like New Year's resolutions, habits are easy to talk about, but much harder to implement. Working together with your partner can help you get over that hurdle.

Describe your ideal vacation.

Is it important to you that we exercise together? If so, what types of physical activities would you like us to engage in as a couple?

When you drive, what do you listen to? Audiobooks, podcasts, music, nothing?

This is another seemingly small question that can really help you and your partner get more in sync. We've all experienced the horror of a passenger reaching for the center console to change the playlist (or even, God forbid, to change the temperature). Married couples tend to travel together a fair amount, and knowing what makes your partner happy when they are behind the wheel can make these journeys as stress-free as possible. You might prefer to listen to music, but if your partner prefers audiobooks, a road trip might represent a great time to pick a book that you can enjoy together.

Do I have any habits that strike you as weird or unusual?

Is there somewhere specific you turn for guidance on living a healthy lifestyle, whether it be an individual, a website, or something else?

What is something important to you today that you believe will continue to be important to you for the rest of your life?

What is something important to you today that you think might not be as important to you in the future?

How often do you think
our home should be "deep
cleaned," and what does a deep
cleaning look like to you?

There's no denying it: cleaning can be a huge hassle. Keeping
your shared environment in tip-top shape is no easy task, and
there's a good chance you and your partner might have different ideas about what constitutes a "mess." Understanding the
level of clutter your partner finds intolerable (and vice versa)
can help put you on the same page when it comes to a
thorough cleaning of your home. Chances are, you're not
scrubbing the toilet every single week, but if you and your
partner can agree that type of chore needs to be done before
company comes over, it helps avoid putting one of you in a
position where you feel like you're always nagging the other
to clean. Agreeing on a set of guidelines, even if they're loose,
can help you and your partner get a bit more in sync.

If you were to create a blog based on an aspect of your life, what would the topic be?

How often would you like to "check in" on our marriage with one another? What form should those conversations take?

It's important to remember that strong relationships don't just happen: they require effort. It isn't always fun to sit down with your partner to take stock of what is working and what isn't, but having an occasional tough conversation will be much better for you in the long run than letting negative emotions fester. It makes sense: if your partner does something that bothers you, it can be hard to know the right time to bring it up. Giving each other an excuse to talk through difficult topics and find a path forward together will help you build a much stronger relationship.

After we moved in together, did you abandon a routine or habit that you miss?

If, starting tomorrow, we were to commit to a new habit together (such as a different bedtime, or the addition of something new, like meditation), what should it be?

Name a bad relationship
habit that you hope
we never adopt.

If we were to queue
up an instructional video
on YouTube to learn a
new skill or technique
together, what would you
want to tackle?

What would a slower pace in our lives look like? How about a faster pace?

Rapid-Fire Round:
Would you rather...

Spend a Friday night out on the town, or cozy at home?

See a live music performance or comedy show?

Play games in which we compete or collaborate?

Cook or bake?

Go to the movies, or lounge with a streaming service?

Climb a mountain or relax on the beach?

Sit at the bar or at a table?

Opposite sides of the booth or same side of the booth?

Go to a concert or a sporting event?

Enjoy a dessert or an extra cocktail at a restaurant?

Be a great chef or a great mixologist?

Have a dog or a cat?

Be an excellent dancer or singer?

Couples Wisdom

"Feeling appreciated is having your spouse do things for you without being asked. Appreciate the things each of you do to make life easier and pleasant for each other. It seems to have worked for 59 years for us."

~John and Jean, married for 59 years

Rapid-Fire Round:

Name an aspect of our daily lives that makes you feel...

Calm / Inspired / Excited / Hopeful
Relieved / Appreciated / Worried / Nostalgic
Desired / Satisfied

SEX AND INTIMACY

Answering intimate questions isn't always easy, and asking them can be even harder. But understanding how to make your partner feel loved when they are at their most vulnerable is one of the most important parts of any relationship. As you navigate your first year of marriage, digging deeper into the quieter, more personal aspects of your relationship can make an already great partnership even better.

How do you see our sex life evolving over the course of our marriage?

What does "quality time" look like to you?

What is quality time? For some, it means curling up in front of the television and enjoying a show together. For others, it means getting out of the house and planning an adventure. Still others might feel most comfortable just sharing the same space, without feeling obliged to engage with one another. Because there are so many different ways in which people prefer to spend their quality time, it is important to set a baseline with your partner. When do you feel the most relaxed? When do they feel closest to you? This doesn't mean that your free time always has to be spent a certain way, but it's always nice to know what makes your partner feel loved and appreciated.

Other than our wedding anniversary, are there other relationship milestones that we should acknowledge or celebrate each year?

What signals do you give when you're in the mood that I may not be tuning in to?

Most of us aren't fully comfortable with the idea of saying something as straightforward as "I'd like to have sex tonight" when we're in the mood. Usually we dance around it—we flirt a little more than usual, or we throw out a subtle signal in the form of a shoulder rub or another form of lingering physical contact. But when your partner doesn't get the hint, it's hard not to feel let down, or even a bit rejected. If you can get on the same page about what your body language is communicating, you'll avoid hurt feelings and find yourselves more in sync when it comes to your nonverbal communication.

What is your preferred time of day to be intimate?

What are your "no-fly zones" when it comes to sex?

Sexual preferences, including likes and dislikes, tend to evolve over the course of a relationship. That's part of the joy of finding someone you're compatible with: trying things you never thought you'd try and discovering new ways to enjoy yourself. But we all have our limits, and it's important to establish clear boundaries that your partner should respect. Communicating with your partner about what you are and aren't willing to try can be awkward at first, but you'll find that opening up those lanes of conversation can be freeing. Partners tend to push each other's boundaries—sexually and otherwise—and that's okay. But respecting your partner's hard limits (and vice versa) will make you both more comfortable exploring everything else.

Is there a fabric type or texture that you find particularly attractive?

What's your favorite
color on me?

What is your favorite
spot in our home
to be intimate?

If you wanted to try something new, would you feel comfortable bringing it up?

Both inside and outside the bedroom, it can be difficult to ask a partner to try something new. For many people, it is even a source of embarrassment. Talking to your partner about how they would prefer to be approached with new or adventurous ideas can help set the stage for clearer communication in the future. True, being open with your partner about your desires is easier said than done. But addressing the topic ahead of time in a neutral way will help both of you feel less "on the spot" when the subject is broached later.

What is your most romantic memory from when we were dating?

Is there anything about our sex life that you worry I talk about with my friends?

Is there anything about
our sex life that
you hope I brag about?

Is there a specific type
of lingerie you find
particularly attractive?

Which is more important to you: verbal affirmation or physical contact?

People prefer to both give and receive affection in different ways. For some people, a small touch on the arm can mean everything. For others, a simple "I love you" or "you look wonderful" can change their whole day. Most people treat their partner the way they themselves like to be treated, but having a discussion about it may highlight differences that can lead to better, more meaningful interactions.

What is the best sex we've ever had?

Do you remember the first time we slept together? What do you remember about it?

When you think about me, what is the first thing you think about?

If we took a random day off from work together, with no other expectations or obligations on our time, how would you want to spend it?

When we go on a date, do you prefer an intimate setting like a fancy restaurant or a vibrant setting like a show or concert?

Is there a romantic moment from a book or film that you'd like us to enact?

When I'm away for an evening or a weekend, what do you miss most?

Has there ever been a time you felt I was the only one you could talk to about something?

Has there ever been a moment when you felt you couldn't trust me?

Sometimes hard conversations are necessary, and a breach of trust doesn't always have to refer to a major incident. For example, if your partner is frequently late—to the point that you no longer believe them when they estimate an arrival or meeting time—that small annoyance can fester into something more. It can often be helpful to have an honest conversation before a minor aggravation can become a major issue.

What romantic clichés do you actually like?

What's your favorite type of kiss?

Do you have a favorite sexual position?

What is your biggest turn off?

Do you prefer giving pleasure or receiving pleasure? Be honest!

When we're apart overnight, is it important to you that we still find a way to say "goodnight" to one another?

What's the hardest I've ever made you laugh?

How quickly are you able to hit the reset button after a fight or difficult conversation?

It can be hard not to let hurt feelings linger when you've had to slog through something heavy together, but tough conversations are only made tougher when you're still off kilter even in the wake of a resolution. Once you've addressed an issue, big or small, in a way that satisfies you both, how do you shake it off so that you don't lose an entire evening to the dark cloud of a now-resolved issue? Sometimes it takes a code word—something as innocuous as the word "pineapple," for instance—to serve as a reminder that life is short, and letting bad feelings gnaw at you only serves to undo the work that you just put into that difficult conversation in the first place.

Do you have a fool-proof way to cheer me up when I'm down?

Do you consider yourself a good secret keeper?

What's your favorite way
I style my hair?

Other than me, in whom
do you confide your
most important secrets?

Do you like telling the story of how we got together? What is your favorite part to share?

What aspects of our private life do you feel should stay completely between us?

Showering together: sexy or annoying?

The "cute" or "romantic" ideas you see in movies or television shows don't always translate to real life. Showering together is just one example of an activity that seems intimate but can wind up being more trouble than it's worth. For some couples, those activities are worth doing anyway, but others might roll their eyes and look for a more practical way to show their affection. Figuring out which camp you fall into can help your partner determine what sort of romantic gestures will resonate with you the most.

Name something, big or small, that your partner does daily that never fails to make you happy.

Couples Wisdom

"In any given disagreement, the 'win' always matters more to one of us. Over the years, we've developed a way to go back and forth and, relatively quickly, determine who 'needs' the win more. We each have things that are more significant and impactful to us, and as soon as it's clear which one of us feels more strongly, the other steps back. Over time, we've discovered it all evens out."

~Cindy and Wayne, married for 16 years

Rapid-Fire Round:
Romantic or Cheesy

Roses / Candles / Poetry / Jazz / Massage oil

A box of chocolates / Silk sheets / Slow dancing at home

Valentine's Day / The phrase "make love"

Rom Coms / Feeding each other finger foods

Love notes / Pet names

Rapid-Fire Round:

One or the Other

Big spoon or little spoon? / Lights on or off?
Music or no? / If yes, what kind? / Dirty talk: turn on
or turn off? / Role playing: yes or no? / Great sex or a
great meal? / Gentle or rough? / Sexting: yes or no?
Physical contact while sleeping: yes or no? / Eye contact,
or eyes closed? / Morning or evening?

Couples Wisdom

"Don't approach a chore or obligation with the mindset that you're
doing so to appease your spouse. When you complete the task, she
will appreciate it more not having to ask for your help, allowing both
of you more time to spend together doing the things you love to do."

~Sam and Andrew, married for 5 years

FAMILY AND FRIENDS

When you got hitched, you and your partner effectively
became your own family unit. Navigating the myriad
expectations imposed on you by parents, relatives, and
friends—no matter how loving their intentions—can be a
challenge. Luckily, there are no rules you need to abide by.
The questions in this section will help you carve your own
path, set boundaries, establish traditions, and continue
getting to know the important figures in each other's lives.

What are the most important traditions that you maintain with your friends?

Which holidays are most important for you to spend with your family?

Do you have any close friends that I haven't met yet?

How often do you want to visit your parents each year, and how frequently should we visit them together?

Prioritizing your partner doesn't mean sacrificing meaningful traditions with your friends and family. For instance, if you and your friends have a long-standing tradition of ringing in the New Year together, there's no rule that you must opt out of meaningful moments with friends just because you're now hitched. As long as you and your partner are clear with one another about what moments you want to mark together—and when you're happy to go your separate ways—proceed with confidence. Don't fall into the trap of doing something as a couple just because it seems to be the "thing to do."

Does hosting
a group of
friends at our
place stress you
out, or sound
like fun?

What is your favorite
activity to do with our
"couple friends"?

Do you feel that you still spend enough time with your close friends now that we're married?

What would you like my relationship with your parents to look like?

The concept of "in-laws" comes pre-loaded with baggage imposed by popular culture and the collective unconscious. But there's no reason that you can't define for yourselves what the term means in the context of your lives together. Does it mean that you visit your in-laws with your partner once a year, or is it important that you form your own relationship with them, independent of your spouse? As with everything, there are no rules. Be open with your spouse about your expectations around both sets of parents—your parents, and your partner's.

Are you closer with your siblings or your friends?

Are there any friends that you have cut out of your life? What caused you to do that?

Have you ever had a falling out with a friend that you wish you could reconcile now, if given the chance?

Is there a "black sheep"
in your family?

What makes you consider
someone a "close" friend?

Do you have an easy time making friends?

Do you go out of your way to keep in touch with far-flung friends?

What are you most grateful to your family for?

Is there anything you resent your family for?

Is there another family that you are particularly close with?

Do I have any friends that you dislike or just don't get along with?

Not all people are compatible, and you shouldn't feel obligated to like every single one of your partner's friends. That said, being honest about why you don't get along with someone is important. After all, explaining that you don't think a certain friend treats your partner very well is a lot different than simply saying "I just don't like her." Sometimes discussing these likes and dislikes can help clear up misconceptions or even help your partner see a friend in a new light. Whatever the case, it's important for your partner to understand that you have a legitimate reason for feeling a certain way.

Do we have any friends with whom you particularly like double-dating?

What do you enjoy/not enjoy about interacting with our friends' children?

Has anyone close to you passed away? How did you handle the grieving process?

Have you ever had to help a friend through a really difficult time?

Do your friends or family members confide in you often?

How many people do you think would consider you their "best friend"?

People tend to put their best foot forward for their partner, which makes sense: you want the person you love to think the best of you. But understanding how your partner is viewed by others in their life can give you a more complete picture of what they are like in their day-to-day life. If your partner has been a groomsman or bridesmaid in a lot of different weddings, or you often find them giving counsel to friends in need, that probably means they are highly thought of within their group of friends. Of course, that doesn't mean it's a bad sign if those things aren't true—some people are naturally quieter or less comfortable offering advice. But it's still a useful rule of thumb to determine whether the person you see in your own life matches the personality your partner projects to others.

Do you think you are good at giving gifts? How do you approach choosing a gift for a friend or family member?

Who was your best friend in elementary school, and are you still in touch? How about high school?

Share a memory about
one of your siblings that
I haven't heard before.

What family trip
do you look back on
most fondly?

What was your favorite book as a child?

Who in your life do you consider to be a mentor?

Who in your family sees you as a role model?

Are there any members of your immediate or extended family whom you'd like to get to know better, or whom you'd like for me to get to know better?

Are there people in our respective groups of friends who haven't met but would get along great if they crossed paths?

Mixing different friend groups is always intimidating, but there's a good chance there are people in your life who would be fast friends if they ever found themselves in the same room. It's a fun thing to think about, especially if you're planning a party or gathering. Don't think of it as playing matchmaker—there doesn't have to be any romantic implications. But hey, it can be hard to make friends as an adult. Getting people with similar interests or personalities together is something that everyone will feel good about, including you.

As we get older, do you see yourself becoming more similar to one of your parents? Does that surprise you?

Is there an area in which you feel competitive with a sibling, or other family member who's close in age?

Does seeing your friends and/or family members interact with their children affect your feelings about having our own kids?

What was your first word?

Is it important to you that I get to know your co-workers? How about your boss?

If we watched home videos from your childhood, is there a specific time, moment, or memory you would want us to revisit together? What would I learn about you?

Tell me a story from your childhood—no matter how mundane—that I haven't heard before.

What are some important qualities that I share with your closest friends?

Is it important to you that
we make new friends
as a couple?

Are there any activities you engage in with your friends that you wish I took part in as well?

Being married doesn't mean that all of your interests need to align; balance is key, so it's important to cultivate hobbies outside of your duo, whether a weekly solo run or a monthly bowling night with work friends. Sometimes, though, you may wish your partner could share in those moments with you. But be thoughtful about what you know your partner does and doesn't enjoy. Don't drag your spouse to hot yoga just because your work friend canceled on you.

Have you thought about names for future children?

If we were to pass down a family recipe, what dish do you think most represents us as a couple?

If I looked through a family photo album from your childhood, what would surprise me most?

If you were to reconnect with an old friend, who would you like that person to be?

How would you describe your role in your main friend group?

Have you ever had to mediate a challenging situation among friends or family? How did you navigate it?

Would your friends describe you as a good listener? How about a good secret-keeper?

Is there anything that you especially admire about the way your parents raised you?

Is there anything your parents did while raising you that you swore you would never do to your own kids?

Rapid-Fire Round:

Would you rather...

Receive a fun gift or a practical gift from a loved one?

Visit friends or family, or have them visit us?

Get together with loved ones over a meal or an activity?

Take a group trip with friends, or with family?

Have a closer relationship with your parents
or with your siblings?

Spend the holidays with family or take a vacation
somewhere far away with just the two of us?

Attend your next high school reunion,
or your next college reunion?

Make friends with our neighbors, or keep to ourselves?

Rapid-Fire Round:
Who is the Person...

I haven't met yet but you most want me to meet?

Whose wedding you are most looking forward to?

You know you can count on for the best advice?

You would call first in an emergency?

You miss the most when you haven't seen them for a while?

Who has helped you the most throughout your life?

You look up to the most?

You know would never judge you?

Who is the most trustworthy with a secret?

Who would always say "yes" to a
spur-of-the-moment invitation?

GOALS AND ASPIRATIONS

When you were single, determining what you wanted out of life was a matter of introspection. Now that you have a committed partner, tackling that question becomes an exciting bit of teamwork as you work to plan your future together. Every day becomes a new opportunity to become a better version of yourself, and help your partner do the same.

What are the most important elements of the geographic area where we settle down?

How much money do you think it's important for us to have in savings?

Think of a friend or family member whose marriage you admire. **What element of their partnership would you like to mirror in ours?**

If we were gifted $10,000 right now, how would you want to spend it?

If we were to learn a new skill together, what should we master?

What are you most looking forward to about our lives together five years from now? How about ten?

What has been your proudest accomplishment in your personal life in the last five years?

How much fulfillment do you need out of your job?

Some of us use the word "vocation" to label what we do professionally, while others derive a sense of meaning from our hobbies and just use our jobs to pay the bills. There's no right or wrong way to engage with work, and everyone is entitled to have the type of relationship with their job that suits them. When you can understand what works best for your partner, then you avoid the risk of imposing your own expectations around your professional life on your spouse. And best of all, you can better understand how to support them through professional transitions and benchmarks.

Money aside, what are some places you'd like to visit together?

If there were no screens in our home, how would we spend our weekend?

If we had a spare room in our home, what would you want to use it for?

What percentage of our income should we set aside for charitable donations each year?

What is your favorite trip
that we've taken together?

How many trips (big or small) would you like to take in a given year?

Is it important to you that we use our vacation days together?

Not everyone views vacation days the same way. Some people see them as an excuse to plan a trip or vacation, while others see them as a way to recharge their batteries by sleeping in and lounging around the house. Figuring out which camp you each fall into can help you plan your vacation days more effectively while making sure your partner is getting what they need out of them. That might mean planning a big getaway to Acapulco, or it might mean letting your partner have a day to themselves without any obligations.

Is there a personal accomplishment (outside of your job) that you hope to achieve within the next five years? How about ten years?

If we collaborated on a big project in our free time together, what would you like to tackle?

If we quit our jobs and opened a business together, what would it be?

How far away are you willing to live from your parents?

What role do you see us playing in our parents' lives as they age?

Nobody wants to think about their parents getting older, but it's important to talk about with your partner. The last thing you want is your in-laws showing up on your doorstep because your partner assumed it wouldn't be a problem caring for them in their twilight years. For some couples, that arrangement works just fine—but certainly not all. Discussing how to care for your parents when they get older—whether that means finding a nearby nursing home for them or simply helping them around the house—is one of those conversations that falls in the "uncomfortable but necessary" category.

If we had a garden, what would you be most interested in growing?

Name something that you've changed your mind about since we first got together.

Is there anything you hope to accomplish that you worry having kids would render impossible?

At what age do you think it would be appropriate to give our kids a cell phone?

Do you ever think about changing careers?
What would you do?

Are there aspects of your parents' partnership that you hope we replicate?

Time and money aside, if you were to go back to school what would you like to study?

If we were to volunteer our time in support of a charity or cause this weekend, what should it be?

Volunteer work is a great way to spend time together while helping to better your community. Learning whether your partner feels drawn to working at a soup kitchen or an animal shelter can not only give you something fun to do together, but it can give you a glimpse into the things that are most important to them. The ways in which we choose to make an impact on the world around us often say the most about who we are as people.

Tell me about a time in the last year that you felt proud of yourself.

How do you want us to celebrate your biggest milestones?

If we engaged in activism, what cause would you like to support together?

Let's set a goal to do a specific activity together once each month for the next year, such as read a new novel together, try a new restaurant, or hike a new trail. What would you like that monthly experience to be?

It can be hard to keep to a daily or weekly schedule, but monthly goals are a lot more attainable, especially when the goal is to do something fun, which gives you something to look forward to throughout the month. What would you be most excited to see on your calendar? Sharing a meal, exploring the world around you, or something else? Even if you are the sort of person who shies away from routines, having a fun activity to plan together is a great way to enjoy some quality time on a regular basis.

How would you like to document our lives together? Do you want to create physical photo albums, or maintain home movies?

If you could become famous for an accomplishment, what would you like to be known for?

Fame is often seen as a goal in its own right, but it can be fun to think about what you would choose to be famous for. More than that, it can be fun to hear how your partner considers the question. Do they zero in on something they know they're good at, or do they choose a more aspirational answer? Either way, it will give you some insight as to how they consider these hypotheticals, and how they think about themselves.

If we had an extra hour to spend together each day, what would you want to do with that time?

What would a child-free life look like for us ten years from now?

Rapid-Fire Round:

Would you rather...

Have a really nice car, or a really nice house?

Live close to your family, or close to your friends?

Have a big house, or a big yard?

Live in the city, or the country?

Have easy access to the mountains, or the ocean?

Learn to ski, or learn to surf?

Have an impressive title at work, or have a
three-day work week?

Be more confident, or more charismatic?

Take more risks, or have a more solid plan for our future?

Be more active, or be more intentional?

Couples Wisdom

"A theater improv approach to marriage can be helpful and fun. Try
tagging the phrase 'Yes, and...' onto most marital statements. It works
when you really want to dig deep into a difficult issue or when you
just want to make sure dessert is included with dinner."

~Chris and Colleen, married for 29 years

Rapid-Fire Round:
Think of your ideal home for us

Does it have more than one floor? If so, how many?

Are big windows important?

What decorative elements are you drawn toward?

Are high ceilings important?

Does it have to have a yard?

Is there a particular color that you love?

What is your preferred style of architecture for a home?

Is there a certain animal or pet you have
always wanted in your home?

If you could only have one or the other:
dishwasher or washing machine?

What needs to be within walking distance?

What is your aesthetic vision for our decor?

How far do you want our home to be from a grocery store?

How far are you willing to live from a public
transportation hub or airport?

Couples Wisdom

"Laughter keeps us balanced. Finding shared humor in life's
highs and lows encourages us to remain on the same team.
Plus, it never hurts to have a few inside jokes!"

~Alyssa and Jide, married for 1 year

QUIRKS AND SCRUPLES

Your partner's charming quirks are a big part of what made you fall for them. They might not be the biggest part of your partner's personality, but they are the little details filling in the edges and creating a more complete portrait of who they are. What do they like to read? Do they hate driving? Have they always wanted to play the clarinet? Most of these questions are on the fun side of the spectrum, but that doesn't make them any less valuable as you learn more about the person you love.

What do you do when you can't sleep?

How do you cope with stress?

Stress is a fact of life, but even so, it can bring out the worst in any of us. Whether you're dealing with a big deadline at work or mediating a conflict between family members, stress chips away at our resilience. It can magnify the minor setbacks and annoyances that we would usually be able to brush off. Suddenly you're throwing up your hands in defensiveness or making a biting comment that you don't really mean. When you're committed to weathering life's ups and downs together—and all of the inevitable stress therein—it's vital to identify not only how your stress manifests, but also your most successful coping strategies. As you start to figure them out, share them with your partner so that you can support each other through stressful periods in a way that works for you.

If I have something serious to bring up, what's the best way for me to do it?

In what ways do you see yourself as the same since we first got together, and in what ways have you changed?

Good partners have the potential to bring out the best in each other. You celebrate each other's best qualities, and the very nature of partnership fosters trust, compassion, generosity, and so many other traits that inevitably make us better people. You've probably even taught each other some important skills in your time together, too—who taught the other the perfect method for cooking that extra crispy bacon you both love? You came together because of who you are at your core, and that hasn't changed, but it's worth taking a step back and acknowledging how you've grown together, too.

What is your favorite snack?

What is your ideal bedroom temperature?

Do you think it is worth paying for organic produce?

When you are
in a bad mood,
how do you
prefer to be
treated?

How are you different at work than you are at home?

What is your favorite space in our home, and why?

How do you signal, consciously or unconsciously, that you need alone time?

What is the most effective way to cheer you up when you're down?

What is your favorite season, and why?

Name your favorite activity in each season.

When you confide a struggle or challenge, do you tend to seek a listening ear, or are you looking for actionable solutions?

What is your favorite
type of cuisine?

What principle or
belief of yours is most
important to you?

Can you work with music playing?

Are pets allowed on the furniture or no?

If you had
to give up
meat or dairy,
which would
you choose?
Could you give
up both?

If you could master any musical instrument, what would it be?

In what ways do you know yourself to be disorganized or forgetful?

Is there a book that you always wanted to read but never had the chance?

What are your ideal pizza toppings?

When you're not feeling well, do you want to be taken care of, or do you want space to recover solo?

There is nothing worse than feeling sick. And when your partner is feeling achy, sniffly, nauseous, or all of the above, it's only natural to want to help them in any way you can. Television and movies have a lot to say on this topic, with suggestions ranging from chicken noodle soup in bed to standing by their side with a box of tissues at the ready. In reality, neither of those seems like a particularly good approach, and you should probably talk to your partner about what actually makes them feel better. Some people just want to be left alone until they have recovered, while others want to be doted on. Both are perfectly normal, just make sure you know your partner's preference.

How do you want your accomplishments acknowledged or celebrated?

Are there things you know you tend to get defensive about?

We all have those "hot button" topics that are hard to approach without heightened emotions. Maybe it's a younger sibling you knowingly indulge too much, or a habit you know you should break. Whatever it may be, when it comes up, your partner's feedback—no matter how cool-headed or even-handed—hits a nerve. It's worth thinking critically about what those topics are for you. You may not be in a place to lower your defenses right now, but being honest about your triggers is a good starting point.

Do you consider yourself to be competitive?

Chore chart: valuable or cringe-worthy?

Do you consider yourself a good multitasker?

What is your biggest nonessential expenditure each month?

Where do you get most of your news?

What is your favorite movie genre?

Is there a type of weather or time of year that affects your mood, either positively or negatively?

When your mind is at rest, what do you find yourself worrying about?

Science fiction or fantasy? Spaceships or dragons?

We all have guilty pleasures, and this can be a nice icebreaker to get your partner to open up about theirs. After all, who doesn't love a good space battle or story about knights on horseback? If you can't even get your partner to admit their true feelings about *Star Wars* or *Game of Thrones*, you may find that you struggle to get them to open up about other things, too.

What's your favorite app on your phone?

What website do you
frequent the most?

Do you believe in
coincidences?
How about fate?

Couples Wisdom

"Marriages are two separate lives entwined together. Life is full of things that can pull a couple apart either physically or emotionally, such as careers, kids, travel, projects, opposing schedules, and obligations. When life gets busy, always find a way to connect with each other for a few minutes each day with a note, a phone call, a text, or photo to remind you both that the other is present."

~Len and Stacy, married for 25 years

Rapid-Fire Round:
High priority or low priority?

Volunteer work

A clutter-free home

Buying local

Staying up-to-date with current events

Your social media presence

A consistent weekly date night

Activism

Spending time outdoors

Getaways, whether close to home or far-flung

Sustainability

Privacy

Gift-giving

Socializing with others as a couple

Clean living

Trying new things

Getting eight hours of sleep

Couples Wisdom

"We really trust, respect, and honor each other. When you say 'I do,'
you need to really mean it. We've been through a lot of sickness
and we care so much for each other that we did everything to make
it okay for the other person."

~James and Kate, married for 63 years

THE HEAVY STUFF

No matter the phase of life or relationship, the unexpected is inevitable. These questions broach topics that aren't necessarily fun to think about, but they're worth tackling together during moments of calm and quiet so that you can face life's challenges together as a united front, if and when the need arises.

Would you rather outlive me, or have me outlive you? Why?

How do you envision your funeral or memorial service? A somber affair, a lively wake, something else? Would you prefer not to have a funeral at all?

Is there one thing that it is important for you to accomplish before you die?

If you only had one year left to live, what would be at the top of your list of things to do, or places to visit?

If you found out you had a terminal disease, with a long and difficult treatment plan and only a slim chance of recovery, would you opt for treatment or choose to live out the rest of your life?

If you were in
a persistent
vegetative state,
would you want
to be kept alive
on life support?
Why/why not?

Do you plan to donate your organs when you die?

If you could know the exact date and time of your death, would you want to know? What do you think would change about the way you live your life if you had this knowledge?

Is there a passage of text you would want read at your funeral, or a song you would want played?

If I passed away unexpectedly, could you see yourself remarrying at some point down the road?

When you pass away, what do you want done with your body? Buried, cremated, shot into space?

About Cider Mill Press
Book Publishers

Good ideas ripen with time. From seed to harvest, Cider Mill Press brings
fine reading, information, and entertainment together between the covers
of its creatively crafted books. Our Cider Mill bears fruit twice a year,
publishing a new crop of titles each spring and fall.

"Where Good Books Are Ready for Press"

Visit us online at
cidermillpress.com
or write to us at
PO Box 454
12 Spring St.
Kennebunkport, Maine 04046